Daphnis and Chloe

John Watson
Daphnis and Chloe

Daphnis and Chloe
ISBN 978 1 76041 949 3
Copyright © John Watson 2020

First published 2020 by
Ginninderra Press
PO Box 3461 Port Adelaide 5015
www.ginninderrapress.com.au

Contents

Book One	11
Book Two	41
Book Three	71
Book Four	99

Foreword

Little is known about Longus except that he wrote *Daphnis and Chloe*, the most famous of the Greek pastoral novels. He probably lived in the second or third century AD. The work has survived in several manuscripts, but it was not until the nineteenth century that a substantial portion from Book One, thought to be missing, was found.

The story of its discovery is a curiosity. While looking at a manuscript in a monastery in Switzerland, Courier chanced upon a passage missing from others and as a result from the translations. He made a copy of it and after completing this task upset his ink – it is said – over the passage. His own copy thus became the only record of the complete text. Goethe claimed that Courier had done this deliberately. In the turmoil of the Napoleonic wars, Courier was assassinated.

Daphnis and Chloe has had numerous translators. The first English version by Angel Daye is very free and manages to incorporate a masque in honour of Queen Elizabeth I. Later English translations seem progressively less lively than the ornate and florid one of 1657 by George Thornley, Gentleman. Those by Jack Lindsay, George Moore, Paul Turner, while exuberant and apparently faithful, seem nonetheless to disappoint expectations raised by the splendid illustrations of Maillol or Bonnard and the ballet of Ravel.

One way to compensate for the flatness of a literal translation seemed to be to attempt a version in verse. The original is in four books with a prologue. This form is retained with a fourteen-line verse throughout, each book having its own pattern, largely alternating arrangements of pentameters, hexameters and heptameters, indented accordingly. It is hoped that with these long lines (despite the metrical dangers usually associated with them in English) something of the charm of the original could be suggested. The translations mentioned above are acknowledged, with particular indebtedness to George Thornley, Gentleman.

Prologue

On Lesbos once while hunting in the woods,
I lost my way before I stumbled on the Grove of Nymphs,
And found a painting there as bright as sunlight on the walls
    Of Herculaneum. It was a frieze

    Which told a pleasant history of love
In all its vagaries, its various hidden joys and tears.
The Grove itself was deep and thick with trees. A fountain played,
    Filling the air with rills, the ground with flowers.

And yet this frieze seemed still more wondrous. In its scenes,
Women gave birth and infants cried. Some were exposed,
While some were wrapped in swaddling. Children tended goats
And others sheep. Thieves lay in hiding. Pirates swarmed –

    These things and more pertaining to love's dangers
    Suggested all that follows and its form.

Book One

1

There was in Lesbos once a lustrous city, Mytilene,
Beside a sea whose glittering canals reflected light
On marble walls and bridges white as cream magnolias.
    Nearby, an estate boasted peaks and plains
All bounded by a curving beach and softly soughing waves,
Whose sigh and susurrus lapped over fields of grazing flocks.
One day Lamon, a goatherd, looking for his animals
Found in a thicket, like a rustic temple made of grass,

A she-goat suckling a child. Her hooves straddled him with care
    While all this time her young were languishing.
Beside the boy-child lay the tokens of his lineage,
A purple cloak fastened with gold, a tiny silver knife.
    At sunset Lamon brought the child back to his wife,
    Who called the boy their own and named him Daphnis.

2

Two years went by. One morning when the gales in the tall trees
        Belied in sound the summer calm below,
        In neighbouring fields a shepherd, in a cave
Made sacred to the Nymphs, found echoes of that suckling goat:

Outside the cave were carvings, in the rock, of Nymphs, their hair
        Floating across their shoulders, arms naked,
        Linen lightly girded round their thighs,
Their faces caught in smiles, as one who dances. From the cave

    There gushed a spume of water flowing in a stream
    About whose entrance flourished lush meadow grass;
    Within the cave hung transverse flutes and pan pipes, reeds,
    The offerings of ancient shepherds to the Nymphs.

        Here Dryas, curious where a ewe, new lambed,
        Had strayed, followed to find a stranger sight.

3

The ewe was nurturing a human child whose milky skin
That nurse licked as the child sucked, at one side, then another,
Greedily feeding like a butting lamb. A girl-child, she
Was, like the other, furnished with rich tokens of high state:
A garland woven with gold thread, a pair of gilded sandals,
    Some anklets wrought from twisted wires of gold.
Then Dryas, learning pity and compassion from the ewe,
Addressed the Nymphs aloud and swore to love their votary,

    And when the shadows stretched beyond the trees,
Returned with his flock and brought the baby girl to show his wife.
    She, Nape, took the child and, strangely moved,
And even jealous of the ewe attending her, agreed
That they should keep the girl, cherish and love her as their own,
    And proudly called her Chloe, a shepherd's name.

4

    The seasons came and, with reluctance, passed.
The children prospered, each waxing in beauty which might seem
To question their inheritance as rustic pastorals.
    Daphnis was fifteen, flourishing like an oak,

    And Chloe two years younger, fair as a birch,
When Lamon and his neighbour, Dryas, had the same strange dream.
In it the Nymphs, once clustered round the cave, stepped down and walked,
    Approaching in a shimmering party, bright,

With hair afloat and naked arms outstretched, pointing
To Daphnis and Chloe standing in a cloud of light.
A child, imperious, a child as they once were
But winged and arrowed, drew back his bow and emptied

    His quiver of its barbs which pierced these two
    Falling as one in one another's arms.

5

And as he charged his bow once more, this boy with butterfly wings,
So confident, so powerful, almost arrogant, decreed
That these his quarries spend their lives in tending goats and sheep.
Lamon and Dryas woke in some dismayed surprise at this;
    (Each hoped for his young child a nobler fate.)
Still, when they met with offerings to that forceful shimmering boy,
They were agreed: Daphnis should herd their goats, Chloe the sheep
    And in a grove they taught them all they knew:

    How animals should graze before high noon,
Or late before dusk falls, and how and when to drive them on
To water or towards their folds, and how to speak to them.
Daphnis and Chloe undertook their work with such delight
There was no doubt that Daphnis had been nurtured by a goat
    And Chloe owed her own life to a sheep.

6

Now spring was every day arriving like some visitor,
>   Apparelled richly, travelling from a south
>   Of fabled fragrance, who in the fields leaves gifts;
On every side, in trees and pastures, flowers multiplied

Until the bees were frazzled and in relays plied their lanes
>   While birds composed fresh changes on old themes
>   And lambs gambolled as if the hills see-sawed
And meadow air divulged again the sweet breath of the past.

> Entranced by spring, like all the world, these tender youths
> Began to imitate whatever danced or sang.
> They heard the trilling of the birds and answered them.
> They skipped like lambs, like bees they visited the flowers.

>> And some they scattered in each other's clothes
>> And some they wove in garlands for the Nymphs.

7

Together in the fields these novices combined their flocks.
They had not ever thought of separating sheep from goats.
And if a sheep ran perilously towards a flooded stream
    It well might be that Daphnis held it back
While Chloe caught cicadas in a cage made out of grass;
And if a goat were clattering near a crest, Chloe might run
To guide it back while Daphnis made a pan pipe out of reeds.
Sometimes one might forget the herds to make some simple toy,

    And then the other, smiling, walked with them.
    They shared the same cool drink of milk and wine,
And every day divided equally their bread and cheese.
    In fact, the sheep and goats which met each day
Were soon as inseparable as Daphnis with his wax reed flute
And Chloe playing with cicadas, caught in her grass cage.

8

    Then while they played, Eros devised events
Charged with a hidden lightning which would irreversibly
Make them his slaves, foregoing other gods. A wolf in cub
        Had raided several flocks from neighbouring fields;

    The villagers dug pits, then covered them
With fronds and leaves, scattering soil about to make it seem
The ground was solid. Yet the wolf was wise and devious,
        And, instead, several sheep and goats were lost

    And Daphnis almost met the same sorry fate:
Some bearded goats were fighting; one with a broken horn
Ran snorting out in pain with Daphnis in pursuit
And in the moment's heat both fell into a pit,

        The goat first, breaking a second horn, and then,
        Breaking his fall on the tumbling goat, Daphnis.

9

Chloe, who had seen them fall, came running to the pit
Where, finding Daphnis still alive, she ran again for help
And brought a nearby herdsman. He began to search for ropes
To haul up Daphnis from the precipice but there were none.
So Chloe then unwound her breast band from her breasts and this
    They lowered into the pit. And Daphnis climbed
Hand over hand to reach the world, while they pulled on the cloth.
The injured goat they raised up too and gave the cowhand. Then,
    Relieved to find their flocks still safe, they sat
    Beneath the leafy branches of an oak.
They searched for injuries but found that fortune smiled on them:
No flowing blood or broken skin; only the bruise-like stain
    Of dirt from the pit. Greatly relieved, they went
For Daphnis to wash himself in the stream that welled from the Nymphs' cave.

10

So, in that sanctuary, he gave his shirt to her to hold
    And stood before the spring and washed his hair,
    And all his body. Chloe watched him wash;
His hair was black and thick, his body sun-browned. Chloe watched.

And then it seemed to her, as if this were the first idea
    Ever to take possession of her thought,
    That Daphnis was more beautiful than she
Had thought. Or rather, never had she thought him beautiful,

    Yet now he was. She helped to wash his back. She found
    His flesh so soft and yielding, yet so finely firm,
    She touched her own skin secretly in disbelief.
    She thought that washing must have made him beautiful.

        And as the sun set, and they led their flocks,
        She wanted now to see him bathe again.

11

Cloudless the next day, Daphnis sat beneath their usual oak
And watched his goats. Clouded, uncertain, Chloe sat with him
And watched her sheep, but more and more watched Daphnis as he played.
For every melody he played today seemed strangely sad
Or joyful as a swallow's cry. Chloe sighed and smiled.
She thought that making music must have made him beautiful
Since, even while she watched him play, that beauty seemed to grow,
    And so she took the flute herself and played.

The sun at noon pierced here and there the oak tree's canopy
    And even in its shade the light seemed fierce.
Thus Chloe in its heat persuaded him to bathe again.
    Again she watched and wondered at his form
    Then reaching out her hand, she touched his flesh,
Praising his beauty. Praise soon blossomed in the spring of love.

12

  Days passed and Chloe did not eat or sleep
And, puzzled, Daphnis noticed that she left her sheep to roam;
And she would laugh and weep in turns, lie down, then suddenly
  Leap up, unable to be still. Her cheek

  Turned pale and then, as soon, was red as flame.
No heifer plagued by gadflies ever grazed more restlessly.
She said, 'I must be sick yet know I am not sick. In pain
  I have no wounds. I grieve, yet lack no sheep.

I burn although I spend the heat of noon in shade.
The brambles and the bees which often stung my arm
Were not as this deep barb. Now I cry out.
  But why? If water or the wash of music made

  Him beautiful, so are the field's flowers.
  His song is sweet, but so are the nightingales'.'

13

'Oh, Sylphs in stone! Could I be that flute, what music I would make.
Alas! You Nymphs, when I must perish from this strange, sweet pain,
    Who then will make you garlands from these flowers,
And who will care for my lambs? And who guard Daphnis as he sleeps?
Or my cicada singing in its cage of woven grass?
Its chirring made me sleep but Daphnis stole all sleep from me.'
    Thus must she speak who had not learned of love,
    Who, nurtured in the Nymphs' cave, asked their help.

That cowherd, Dorcon, who had helped haul Daphnis from the pit,
Knew something of these things. His beard already grew somewhat
And on this very day he fell in love with Chloe. She
Loved Daphnis without knowing why. But Dorcon was inflamed
    And sought by any means to win the prize.
At first he hoped with gifts each day to grow in Chloe's eyes.

14

To seem the friend of both he gave Daphnis a nine-quilled pipe
        Bound up with brass rather than wax; to Chloe,
        Such a doe-skin as the Bacchantes wear,
Dappled and brightly marked as if in colours just for her.

And gradually he chose to exclude Daphnis and bring only
        Gifts for Chloe, a fragrant cheese, a posy
        Of field flowers, early summer apples,
And even once, a newborn calf, a goblet laid with gold,

    Some fledglings from a mountain nest. Chloe was pleased,
    But only, knowing nothing of love's wiles, because
    She then could give these gifts to Daphnis. So at last,
    For Eros soon intended Daphnis to be bound,

        A contest of words the two young men devised
        For Chloe's kiss, with Chloe as the judge.

15

This agon in the fields began. Dorcon spoke first. 'I am
Taller than Daphnis, and a cowherd. Cows are to goats
As I to Daphnis, that is, superior. I'm white as milk.
    My hair is red as corn at harvest time.
What's more, my mother nursed me, not some wandering mountain goat.
So he's as much a kid as these here under this shadowy oak.
Daphnis is beardless as a girl, and dark as any wolf.
    And while he tends the goats he smells like them.'

Dorcon repeated much of this and then yielded the stage
To Daphnis who began, 'It's true a she-goat suckled me
But so was Zeus raised – let us not forget that fact. And then,
    The goats I graze are bigger than his sheep
And I deny they smell. For Pan, himself three-quarters goat,
    Does not. And Dionysus has no beard.
I'm dark, but so are hyacinths. His beard is red as a fox.'

16

'And so,' said Daphnis warming to the task,
'If you should kiss, at least you kiss my mouth and not a beard
As if you kissed a fox. And don't forget in judging this
    You were yourself raised by a ewe and you

    Yourself, and even so, are beautiful!'
Chloe, perhaps swayed by this compliment, and also since
She'd wanted for a long time to be kissed by Daphnis, cried
    That he had won. Dorcon ran off at once

As Daphnis had his prize. Without a moment's pause
She kissed him artlessly not knowing how. And yet
It was a kiss in which he felt the circling bands
Of Eros tighten round him. As he gazed he knew

    He had been blind: Her hair was gold as fire,
    Her eyes like grazing beasts', her skin like milk.

17

And now it was the goats who were neglected. Daphnis fell
>   Into a lethargy. He scarcely ate,
>   He spoke only to Chloe or himself.
He pondered: 'Could that kiss have poisoned me? And if so, how
Could she herself not have succumbed? It is a mystery:
Her lips are soft as roses and more sweet than honeycomb
Which bees have hidden in the meadows. Yet they caused me pain,
A pain so sweet my heart leaps to my mouth, longing again.

How wantonly and free of care the goats play in the field
While I am idle. How delightful are the nightingales
While I have thrown aside my pipes. And how remote and bright
>   The violet, cowslip and the hyacinth,
>   While still I make no garlands, waiting Chloe.'
But Dorcon, meanwhile, brooded on dark plans to win the prize.

18

He went to Dryas with more gifts of cheese and eggs and milk
        And, making much of friendship, turned their talk
        To Chloe and his hopes of marrying her,
Adducing then this generous inventory of nuptial gifts:

A yoke of oxen for the plough, a grove of apple trees,
        Four hives of bees, a hide for making sandals,
        The promise of a weaned calf every year.
Thinking of Chloe's future happiness, Dryas declined.

    Dorcon had failed again (and wasted cheese and eggs)
    And now determined to use force. He would become
    A sheep in wolf's clothing. He took a wolf's skin
    And wore it like a cloak, his head within the pelt.

        Then at the spring he hid till Chloe came
        Alone, while Daphnis cut the goats fresh leaves.

19

But when he hoped to carry Chloe off subdued in fears,
The dogs (who are a nuisance always, sniffing everywhere)
Discovered him and in his thicket leaped and snarled and bit
Until he had to shriek for help and Daphnis called them off.
Then he and Chloe led him to the spring and bathed his wounds
And chewed green elm bark to a soothing paste which they applied,
    While laughing at what they thought a pastoral joke:
How strange the world which sees a wolf snatched from the jaws of dogs!

Meanwhile their barking and the sight of a disgorging wolf,
    These loud alarms had frightened all the herds
To tremble on the rocky crags or run beside the sea.
    And so their world was still turned upside down
When, Dorcon gone, the two must clamber over rocks to find
    Their scattered flocks at last, and drive them home.

20

    That night their tiredness eased the pain of love
And both slept deeply. Yet at sunrise when they woke, they knew
Only that Chloe seeing Daphnis bathing at the spring
        And Daphnis by that single kiss were bound

    As certain trees are draped in shedding bark
Or willows tangled in their wands. And summer swelling all
The crops and creatures in the fields increased this tyranny
        Of Eros over them. The meadows sang,

The murmuring locusts and the sounds of bleating sheep
Whispered that love caused fruit to fall and lie in grass,
The breezes found each opening in the hedge and sweetly
Carried there the smell of quince and pear. The sun,

    Beside himself with love for beauty, urged
    That everyone undress and meet his gaze.

21

    Daphnis, inflamed, swam in the cooling stream
    And drank its welling flood to quench that fire.
When Chloe finished making cheeses, having to contend
With summer flies, she washed, and crowned her head with sprigs of pine
And wore her doe-skin, making for them both a syllabub
Of wine and milk. Each was a prisoner in the other's eyes
And many days they spent in this sweet cage. Daphnis would seize
From Chloe's head the pine-wreath, kissing and wearing it himself,

And when he bathed and Chloe watched, she sometimes wore his clothes.
    And once they threw green apples at each other;
Then they laughed and smoothed each other's hair. His was so black
She said it was like myrtle berries. Then he said her face
    Was like a summer apple, pink and white.
And if she played his pipes, by touching them he touched her mouth.

22

Their flocks lay in the shade. Chloe slept. Daphnis gazed.
    Although he cried, 'What lips! What sleeping eyes!'
    He dared not kiss her since that made him drunk
Like honey new from the bees; besides, he wanted her to sleep.

The field was filled with noise. And still she slept. Then suddenly
    A grasshopper beating skittish yellow wings,
    Pursued by a swallow, escaped into her dress.
The bird's wing brushed her face and so she woke and cried aloud

    And smiled. Then Daphnis plunged his hands between her breasts
    And, conjuring, produced the insect like a twig;
    But Chloe took it back, caging it in her hands
    And placed it once more in the safety of her breast.

    Again the ringdoves sounded distantly
    And Daphnis told the tale of their complaint.

23

    'This is the ringdove's story,' Daphnis said.
'Once upon a time there was a beautiful young girl
Who grazed her cows in the mottled woods. They knew and loved her voice.
She sat beneath the pine and garlanded herself with twigs
    And sang of Pan. Nearby, a handsome boy
Sang even more persuasively, making eight of her flock
    Cross a narrow stream to graze with his.
So hurt was she this summer day at losing both her flock

    And her much vaunted eminence in music,
That she approached the gods and begged them by their sacred power
To change her to a bird with all the advantages of song
And flight above the flocks. The gods agreed and she became
This bird that haunts the hills and woods with voices like a girl's.
And still she sadly sings and calls her truant wandering cows.'

24

Such were their summer pleasures. But when autumn
Coloured first the grapes, then many trees and stubble fields,
Some Tyrian pirates in a stolen vessel reached their coast
    And, armed with swords, plundered their fragrant stores,

    Their wines and grain, their precious honeycomb,
Some cows from Dorcon's herd. But soon they saw a greater prize
And seized and dragged off Daphnis from the shore into their boat,
    Untied the mooring-rope and put to sea.

Chloe was driving out her flock. She heard her name
Called loudly from the sea. She knew Daphnis' voice
And ran to Dorcon in the field. But he, alas,
Lay where the pirates left him mortal in his wounds.

    He cried, 'Play on this pipe. The stolen cows
    Will know the sound and come. Remember me.'

25

And Dorcon died as Chloe kissed him gently. Then she seized
The pan flute, thinking only of Daphnis, and ran towards the shore.
Facing the sea, loudly she played the tune Daphnis had taught her.
The cows responded violently and leaped, all from one side,
      Into the sea. A trough gaped near the boat
Then, flooding back, capsized it, throwing Daphnis overboard.
The thieves, weighed down with swords and metal breastplates, quickly drowned.
But Daphnis slipping from his clothes swam in between two cows

And seized their horns, one in each hand, and thus attained the shore
      With ease, as though he drove a chariot;
For oxen swim prodigiously, almost as well as fish
      Or waterfowl. Thus Daphnis had escaped
      Both shipwreck and the pirates. Safe on land,
In Chloe's arms he heard (except for the kiss) of Dorcon's fate.

26

On Dorcon's grave they built a mound and planted fruit trees there.
> Clusters of grapes they crushed and poured with milk
> Over the ground they strewed with broken flutes.
From all the fields there came the lugubrious bellowing of beasts

Who, shuddering, drew near to honour Dorcon by their cries.
> Then Chloe led her Daphnis to the cave
> And washed him at the spring. She paused and smiled,
Then for the first time naked to his gaze she washed herself,

> Whose body was so white, so beautiful, it seemed
> That she should never wash at all, nor ever dress.
> They gathered flowers from the beds of summer blooms
> And wove them into chains and garlands for the Nymphs.

>> At last they came away and sought their flocks,
>> Who waited patiently for their return.

27

But Daphnis had seen Chloe naked. And while the goats and sheep
    Seemed joyful at their return and grazed again
And frolicked when they heard once more the music of the pan flute,
Daphnis had seen Chloe naked at the Nymphs' own pool.
And so he viewed that general happiness across a gulf
    As if a poison ate into his heart;
To breathe was difficult, sometimes as if he were pursued.
Sometimes he scarcely breathed at all, and all because

He had seen Chloe at the spring where all that once was hidden
Now proclaimed her person. Joy mixed with perplexity;
The pool seemed now more dangerous than the dark capsizing sea.
    He had escaped to be a captive still
For he was young and lived in rustic shades and, ignorant,
    Knew nothing of the Piracy of Love.

Book Two

28

    Autumn announced itself with radiant skies;
And pale and dark grapes clustered on the vines, hidden in leaves.
No one was idle. Some prepared the wine-press, some the jars,

    Some gathered baskets, some made sickles, some
Brought stones to crush the berries. Others were making willow flares
To light the workers drawing sweet must from the press at night.
Daphnis and Chloe left their flocks to help in the great vintage.
While Daphnis carried baskets from the vines, and trod the press,
    Chloe poured wine for everyone who worked.

    Some women kissed this Dionysian Daphnis,
Just as the men who trod the grapes called Chloe their Bacchante.
These would-be satyrs said they wished they all were Chloe's sheep,

    That she might be their shepherd and lead them with her crook.
The first event made Daphnis smile; the second, Chloe.

29

    The vintage with its revelries had passed.
Daphnis and Chloe had returned once more to lead their herds
Alone on to the plains. That evening they addressed the Nymphs
    And brought them grapes attached to leaves and vine.

    While they were singing to their animals,
An old man wearing goatskins came and, sitting down, began
To talk to them at great length in the oak tree's lengthening shade:
'My children, I am Philetas. And many the song I've sung
To the Nymphs and many the tune I've piped great Pan, and many the herds
I've led with music alone. But now I'll tell you why I've come.

    I have a garden which has made me very proud.
    In spring there are roses, hyacinths and violets,
    In summer, poppies, pears and many kinds of apples.
Now there are grapes and figs and pomegranates. But I digress –'

30

'The birds assemble there to eat or sing.
It's watered by three springs and bounded by a wall of vines.
Today at noon I saw again the same startling boy,

As white as milk, his hair as gold as fire,
His naked body bright as if he'd just been bathing. Well,
He played amongst my pomegranates and my myrtle fruit,
His cheeks as bright, his hair as black as they. Capricious boy!
I rushed to catch him lest he break my heavy-laden boughs,

But like a pheasant chick he hid in leaves.

I was tired now and leaning on my staff.
I asked him who his mother was and where he'd come from. Then
He softly laughed and threw some myrtle berries in my path.

I don't know why, but I too smiled and gave him fruit.
Despite myself I asked him for a single kiss.'

31

'At that he laughed in such a voice as never nightingale
        Nor swan could emulate. He cried, "Of course!
If so you wish. For I like being kissed at least as much
As you would like not to be old. But is it really wise?

        Your age will not prevent your wanting more
And I am hard to catch. Not even hawks or eagles match me
In the air. For I am not a child. I am as old
        As Time itself and all the universe.
I knew you when you were a youth. I watched you grazing cows
Beside the water-meadow. When you played to Pan I heard,

    And when you longed for Amaryllis it was I
    Who brought her to your nuptial bed. She bore your son.
    I stood beside you then. But now my chief concern
    In all this world is Chloe and her Daphnis."'

32

    '"I bring them to the fields and see each gaze
Fill and dissolve the other's for the day. And then I come
To bathe and rest in your fine garden. That is why your trees

    And flowers flourish – poppies, myrtles, pears –
All have been splashed with water from my bathing in your springs
Like colour splashed with light. Now look about. See for yourself
That not a single branch or fruit or petal has been bruised.
No other person in the world has seen me at your age
    So you should be well pleased." At this he sprang

    Into the myrtles like a nightingale
And skipped from bough to bough. Through leaves I caught a glimpse of wings
And, as he vanished, a quiver slung between his shoulderblades.

    I came straightway to tell you that your happiness
By Eros seems assured, your lives linked in his hands.'

33

    Daphnis and Chloe smiled and Chloe asked,
'But who is Eros?' And the old man smiled. 'My children, Eros
Is a god in love with youth and beauty. But he has power
        Over the stars and over other gods.

    All creatures are impelled and led by him.
The flowers are his instrument; he makes the rivers flow.
I even knew a bull once who would bellow in his straits.
When I was young and fell in love with Amaryllis, he
Ensured I could not sleep, nor eat nor drink. Perhaps you know.
My body was like ice, my heart on fire. I see you do.

    I cried to Pan who'd known love, and Echo who
Repeated Amaryllis' name each time I spoke.
    I broke my flute because it brought the cows not her.
I found that Eros gave no cure for all he brought of love.'

34

'Perhaps the only remedy is to kiss,
Embrace and lie together naked.' Here he paused for breath
And smiled at them. They thanked him for his news and so he left

With gifts of cheese and a kid with budding horns.
At this a strange excitement held them. They had never known
The name of Eros. All that they now heard matched all they'd felt.
They too had known that fire and ice and longings for that pain.
(That flying bird-like boy must be the same their fathers saw
 In dreams, who ordered them to graze their flocks.)

'What can we do,' cried Daphnis, 'we who love?
The Nymphs might help us. But the spell is strong. And even Pan
Could not help Philetas. We'll have to trust the remedies

He spoke about: To kiss and then embrace and then,
Despite the cold, to lie down naked on the ground.'

35

    The following day soon after dawn they met
And, once their flocks were grazing and secure, they ran to try,
In a kind of furious impatience, kissing as their cure;
        Then locked in one another's arms they strove

        To ease their pain, assuage their thirst and quench
The flame that would not melt the ice still coursing in their veins.
In vain. This happiness, calamitous as mortal pain,
This suffering as sweet and dense as layered honeycomb
Would not respond to either of the first two remedies
        Despite the fervour of their trials. And yet,

Something still made them hesitate to try the third resort.
    They spent a sleepless night, each pondering what they'd done
    And what they'd left undone. But in their dreams they lay
    In flooding light together naked on the ground.

36

    The sun rose late and, as they reached the fields
A frost still covered all the clefts and rills. Their flocks were calm
But they were violently impelled towards those remedies

    Although uncertain still about the third.
They smiled and seriously began again those measures which
So far could not allay the pains of love. Thus still they hung
In the glistening net of Eros. Kisses and embraces failed.
Therefore, they reasoned, lying side by side on the cool ground
    Must be the means to ease their troubled joy.

    And yet instead, they kissed more eagerly
As if to bruise and bind each other, each in the other's arms,
Might still deliver them from Eros. Then by accident

  As they embraced, they fell. As Chloe turned her head
  And Daphnis followed, soon they lay as in their dreams.

37

    Yet innocent of what to do they lay
Outstretched, still partly clothed, but as the remedy required,
With limb on limb, and waited for the cure. Perhaps had they
    Remained thus, Eros may have seen and flown

    And in a sudden lightning taught them all
They did not know. But Nature was distracted by events
Which soon would interrupt their pastoral pleasures in the fields,
And equally the turbulence of love, in which these two
    Trudged homeward with their flocks that painful night.
It happened in the following way. Some rich young wayward men

On holidays from Methymna sailed up and down the coast
    Where there are many bathing pools, gardens and woods.
    They fished and hunted where they moored. Sometimes their dogs
    Caught hares escaping from the vineyard's sudden noise.

38

    And sometimes they caught fowl, wild geese and ducks
To stock their table. So they sailed serenely down the coast.
They seemed harmless enough, were generous with local people

    Whenever they bought bread and wine or lodgings.
(As autumn passed they beached the yacht at night for fear of storms.)
But now, a curious event: a peasant needing rope
To haul a vintage stone approached the sleeping ship and stole
Its mooring rope; those sailors in the morning searched and swore
    But sailed at last to the fields of Daphnis and Chloe.

    They made a cable there of willow wands
While their eager dogs leaped to the shore and, running on ahead,
Disturbed the goats. These ran downhill towards the anchorage

  And gathered near the yacht. One bold and hungry she-goat
  Ate the tie which held the rocking ship to land.

39

    The wind blew from the mountains and the waves
Stood resolute before they fell. The swell grew stronger still,
Until the yacht was set adrift and in the billowing backwash
Carried out to sea. The Methymneans with their hounds

Came running back and from the futile shore watched as their ship
Vanished from sight. Dismay next turned to rage which drove them back
To find the careless herdsman of the hawser-eating goats.
Confronting Daphnis, they accused then beat him violently.
But Lamon came with Dryas to his aid, calling a halt,
      Insisting on a fair, impartial trial.

  Philetas as the village elder was made judge.
  The injured party roundly spoke its grievances:
  Some goats of the defendant ate their mooring cable;
Because of this they lost a ship and precious cargo, clothes,

40

  Dog harness, silver equalling in worth
The estates of this wretched Mytilene. 'And thus we claim
As forfeit this incompetent whose goats he grazed on sand

  Instead of in the fields. We rest our case.'
Daphnis, still bloodied from their battering, saw Chloe's face
And bravely spoke in his defence. 'My lords, it's very clear
My goats were harried by these people's hounds to leave their field.
Of course they ate their rope. Goats can't eat sand. There was no grass

  Or strawberry tree or thyme there on the beach.

  And who's incompetent? Look at my goats.
You see how beautiful they look. I think it's obvious
I care for them more prudently than they control their dogs.

 And who would leave a ship, loaded with valuables,
Attached to the land by nothing more than osiers?'

41

    'Besides,' said Daphnis, 'waves and wind, not goats
Were what bore off their boat. So blame the weather. Don't blame me.'
At this, poor Daphnis burst into tears and won the sympathy
Of all the crowd. Philetas swore by Pan,

    And by all the Nymphs presiding at the field,
That Daphnis and his goats were singly and collectively
Quite innocent, and that the sea and winds were guilty, but
These came within the jurisdiction of another court.
The crowd applauded this summation of the case and cheered.
The travellers were not convinced. They flew into a rage

And seizing Daphnis tried once more to drag him off.
    But now the villagers joined in and put to flight
    These sorry voyagers, who, now pedestrians,
    Yachtsmen no more, at length reached Methymna.

42

    Meanwhile, through all this scuffling, Chloe led
Her wounded Daphnis to the cave and gently washed his face
So cruelly smeared with blood. Next she produced some bread and cheese

    And, seated by the fountain, made him eat.
Then even more restorative, yet dangerous, was the kiss
Like honey from her lips. That this might be the end of all!
But worse was still to come from those ill-fated travellers.
At length, reaching their homes in Methymna, they showed their wounds
    And said their yacht was seized by force of arms

    Stirring those citizens to seek revenge
So that next day a general led a force of ten armed ships
Towards the enemy coast and plunder there. They raided fields

    Where Daphnis grazed his flocks, they seized fresh wine and corn
    And sheep and goats, but one far fairer prize remained.

43

    Daphnis was in the woods, cutting green leaves
As winter fodder. He saw the raiding party from the trees
And hid. But while he waited in a hollow beech tree's cave,
    Chloe, with her flocks, saw men approach.

She ran to the Nymphs for sanctuary, then begged her capturers
In their most sacred name to spare her and her animals.
But these Methymneans laughed at such stone images, and with force
Impelled her like the sheep and goats with whips of willow wands,
Then, filling their ships with plunder, sailed away, fearing a storm
    And retribution from their enemy.

    Daphnis now ventured to the fields. Chloe was gone.
    Her pan pipe lay on the ground. He ran to the cave and cried,
    'Oh Nymphs, how could you watch Chloe and all our flocks
        Abducted? Chloe gone! What shall I do?'

44

    Daphnis continued in this way until,
Exhausted by his grief, he fell into a curious sleep.
He dreamed the three Nymphs stood before him, tall and beautiful,

    Half-naked, barefoot, with their hair set free,
Serene as in the carvings. One said, 'Daphnis, do not now
Reproach us. For we feel as much concern as you. Your Chloe
Was nurtured in our cave when first she was abandoned. So
We have petitioned Pan (whom, incidentally, you yourself
    Have much neglected with your fruit and flowers.)

    For he is used to wars and we are not.
Great Pan is now resolved to intervene on her behalf.
But you are missed and must return to Lamon and Myrtale

  Who think you lost. Your Chloe will return. But then
  The tasks that Eros sets will still be yours to solve.'

45

    In tears of grief and joy and gratitude
Daphnis leaped up from sleep and ran to the aromatic pine,
Deep within whose scented shadow Pan stood, horned and hooved,
    Holding a pan flute and a dancing goat.

    At dusk, his overture to the gods complete,
He thought of Lamon and Myrtale waiting fearfully
And hastened with his leaves back to the welcoming cottage. Night
For him that night seemed endless. Yet elsewhere the night was filled
With sudden strange events and portents. In a protected harbour
    The Methymneans anchored for the night,

  Where from their revelries the whole sea seemed on fire;
  The sound of oars announced invisible attacks.
  Confused, they ran on deck. It seemed their ship was flung
Into a great night-battle with an unseen enemy.

46

    This strange and dreadful night was followed by
A stranger dawn. Chloe stood at the mast crowned with pine;
About the horns of Daphnis' goats grew flowering ivy trails,

    While stolen cows and calves made howls like wolves.
The anchors seemed impossible to raise, the oars like straw,
Dolphins in the waves dislodged the planking from the prow,
From somewhere in the cliffs shrill pan pipes pierced the air like trumpets.
All was confusion. Then the general fell into a sleep
    In which great Pan himself appeared and said,

    'Impious mortals! By what right have you
Brought war upon these fields so dear to me and driven away
The flocks that grazed under my care. Not only this but worse:

  You ravished from the altar of the Nymphs that maid
  Whose story is the work of Eros still untold.'

47

    The pan flute still like trumpets shrilled and rang.
The general woke in fear and looked for Chloe on the deck,
Her hair still wreathed in pine. He ferried her himself to shore,
    At which the pan flute sounded pastorally

    Across the waves. On board, amongst the herded animals
As if called home, her sheep ran down the gangway, and the goats
Climbed nimbly down the ladders to the sea and swam ashore.
Her flocks all clustered round her in a joyful dance. She watched
The Methymnean ships begin to sail away; the anchors
    Weighed themselves, while dolphins led the way.

    Once more the herd grazed calmly in the field.
Daphnis watched from the cliffs as Chloe came ashore
And cried aloud, 'Oh Nymphs! Great Pan!' and ran like the wind,
    Already breathless into her embrace.

48

    The ivy on the goats, the fire at sea,
The noise of oars invisible, the howls of calves, her fears,
The trumpet from the cliff, the pine wreath in her hair, his hopes,

    His dream of the Nymphs and Pan, his happiness:
All that had passed they told each other sitting near the oak
And planned the tributes they must make, both to the Nymphs and Pan:
Libations, garlands and a sacrifice, a goat entwined
With ivy such as Chloe had described. For all of these
    Lamon and Dryas and their families

    Came to the woods. They sang songs to the Nymphs
And ate and drank. And Daphnis played his flute and Chloe danced.
Then Philetas arrived with flowers with which to garland Pan.
    At length with wine and boasting they beguiled the time;
    Some talked of pirates, some of wolves, and some of youth.

49

    As Philetas was boasting of his skills
At playing the pan flute, equalled only by great Pan himself,
Daphnis began to urge him to instruct them. Philetas

    When urged again agreed at last (although
He said, he was too old and short of breath to excel).
They gave him Daphnis' pipe but it, he said, was far too small
To do his talents justice and was really only fit
For a boy to play on. So his son, gambolling like a kid,
Was sent to fetch a proper pipe, a worthy instrument,
    One fit for Pan himself. The boy threw off

His coat and, naked, ran to his father's house.
Meanwhile Lamon agreed to tell the Tale of the Pipe
Which once Sicilian shepherds had relayed to him
    In return for such a pipe and his finest goat.

50

    'You may not know this, but originally
This pan pipe that we know so well was once a beautiful girl
With an unusually charming voice. She used to graze her goats

    And play amongst the Nymphs and sing. One day
Pan saw her and to talk her into answering his desire,
He promised he would make each pair of goats she had have twins.
She laughed and said she could not give herself to one who was
Neither a goat nor a man. He chased her to the reeds. She hid
    And Pan slashed at the reeds but found no girl.

    She had quite vanished. Then he bound some reeds
And fastened them with wax. He made them of unequal length
Since love had proved unequal. Then he brought them to his lips,

    And thus the pan flute, such a one as Philetas
    Will shortly play, was once a breathing lustrous girl.'

51

    As Philetas praised Lamon for this tale
His red-haired son returned. The pan flute which he held was large
And fine and bound in bronze, almost the very instrument
Pan made himself. So Philetas sat upright on a bench

    And spent some time examining the reeds,
Before he started in a loud and robust tone to play
So powerfully that it seemed like several flutes sounding at once.
Then gradually he played a sweeter tune, like distant birds,
And ranged through pastoral music of all kinds until he reached
    The style of music suitable for cows.

  For cows the tone was loud. Next came the tune for sheep,
A lulling gentle sound, and finally the tone
  Which one would use for goats, a shrill and thrilling cry.
    In short, he gave them flutes from round the world.

52

    The company sat entranced. Then Dryas rose.
Impatiently he asked for Dionysian music. Then
He danced his famous wine press dance or epilenion,

    In which he mimed the picking of the fruit,
The treading in the press, the filling of jars and finally
The savouring of new wine. So ardently did Dryas dance,
That everyone saw vines and fruit, and smelt the fragrant press,
And drank the sweet fermenting juice. Then Daphnis leapt to his feet
    And taking Chloe's hand assumed the stage:

    'We give you Pan and Syrinx, Lamon's tale'
And so they danced. While Chloe sang, Daphnis, as Pan, approached,
Gently at first, then passionately, on his toes suggesting hooves.

  Chloe hid and Daphnis played a plaintive tune.
  At last the two embraced, as if their play were real.

53

    And when the sun was lost behind the pine,
Old Philetas made Daphnis keep the flute, to give in turn
To his successor. Then, reluctantly, they all dispersed
        And Chloe called her sheep and Daphnis his goats.

    And in that dusk they were alone again
Resolving, as they walked together slowly home, to meet
Soon after dawn the following day. And this they did. Of course,
They first made offerings to the Nymphs and then to Pan. They kissed,
And next embraced, then lay together on the open ground.
        Uncertain still, they drank milk mixed with wine.

  Inflamed, they vied with one another in their boasts
  And protestations of their greater love. Each swore
  By all the gods to love the other endlessly,
      Yet Chloe voiced some doubts on Daphnis' vows:

54

    For Daphnis at the pine swore fervently
By Pan that he would not survive a single day alone,
Bereft if taken from his Chloe. Chloe to the Nymphs

    Swore too that all she wanted in this world
Was just to live and die with Daphnis. But she felt unease:
'Daphnis,' she said, 'You know that Pan to whom you swore your oath
Is always falling in and out of love. There was the girl
Changed to a pine. There was the girl changed to a flute. There was
    A host of wood nymphs he always pursued;

    So if you swear by him…I think you see.
Swear by this herd of goats, and by the goat who suckled you,
Never to leave your Chloe who is true always to you.'

    Daphnis was charmed. He seized a goat in either hand
And swore. Shepherds, she thought, should swear by goats or sheep.

Book Three

55

When Mytileneans heard of the attacks
And plunder of their crops and animals, they were outraged
And raised a force of infantry and cavalry to march
On Methymna, since winter kept their fleets safe in their bays.

    Led by Hippasos they declined to plunder fields
    Or rob the peasants, for this seemed like piracy
        Rather than war. Instead, outside the walls

    Of Methymna they camped, and heralds came
    To sue for peace since, they explained, their citizenry
    Had not been party to those first attacks. At length

Hippasos, sending word of this to Mytilene, then heard
That he should accept the peace, provided all their plundered goods
Be safely, and in full, returned. For Mytilene had judged
    Peace to be far more provident than war.

56

    Thus ended war between these neighbouring states
As unexpectedly as it began. And in its place
Winter advanced, which was for Daphnis and Chloe even worse.
For suddenly a fall of snow had blocked the roads. The woods
Could not be crossed. The trees bent low, bearing their heavy load,
      And no one drove their flocks or went outdoors.

    Instead great fires were lit indoors. The day
Was spent in spinning flax and weaving nets to take to sea,
Or combing and carding goat hair for the loom, or making snares
For birds who stole from the crops. And there were animals to feed.
The pigs had acorns, cows had chaff, and goats green leaves from the loft.
Most shepherds saw this as a holiday, to sleep till late,
   To eat a meal then spend the day at work indoors.
   But Daphnis could not graze his goats with Chloe's sheep.

57

    A wall of glass now sealed their cave. The Nymphs
Stood indistinctly in a fall of ice. Snow filled the grove
While Chloe learnt the desolate art of carding wool at home.
A shoulder bag in which she'd brought him food, a milk pail, one

    They'd drunk from when the fields were warm, an idle flute
    Which in the summer he had played to her, all these
        Seemed only to enhance their loneliness.

    But Daphnis thought of ways despite the snow
    To visit Chloe: outside Dryas' cottage grew
    Two myrtle trees with ivy interlaced between,

So as to make a sort of tent or cave in which there hung
Clusters of berries large as grapes suspended from each branch.
Birds gathered there in winter, blackbirds, starlings, pigeons, thrush,
    Those twittering flocks which feed on ivy fruit.

58

    So one day Daphnis set out through the snow.
He took his snares, his bird lime, threads and nets, his honey cakes,
Ostensibly in search of birds. A mile of hidden paths,
Which in their summer had enticed them, now lay under drifts,
Almost impassable. Yet love will often find a way
    Through fire and water, even Scythian snows.

    And so at last he reached the myrtle trees,
Set all his snares, affixing bird lime to the trembling wands,
Then waited hopefully. The birds arrived but no one stirred
From Chloe's cottage. Baffled, Daphnis looked for some excuse
To knock and in this wilderness of snow seem plausible.
'I've come to ask for fire.' 'Why come so far?' 'For bread –'
    'Your bag is filled with food.' 'We needed wine.' 'So soon
    After the vintage?' 'A wolf chased me.' 'Where are its tracks?'

59

    Although his bag was soon quite filled with birds
He still might not see Chloe till the spring unless he thought
Of some excuse which, if he knocked, might not seem too absurd.
Then Eros who is watchful, even through cold winter's snow,

    Invented this diversion so that Daphnis would
    At once see Chloe in the warmth of Dryas' house:
        Inside, the meat was being carved, and bread

        And wine passed round the table. Suddenly
    One of the sheep dogs leapt and seized some meat and ran
    Out through the door. Dryas cried out, (It was his plate)

And plunged into the snow in hot (but very cold) pursuit.
When, at the ivy, Daphnis stumbled out about to leave,
His loaded bag high on his shoulder, Dryas laughed and called,
    'Good day, my boy. You must be cold! Come in.'

60

    Daphnis again on gazing Chloe gazed
And each of them like young trees in a wood withstood the snow
Of greetings falling round them, stood upright and smiled and then
Embraced and kissed, as courtesy allowed them both to do.
Daphnis produced the thrush and blackbirds from his bag, and talked
    Of myrtle, ivy, berries, birds, the snow.

    They offered Daphnis meat (or what was left
After the dog had finished his.) And Chloe brought him wine,
First sipping from the cup herself before she passed it on.
Daphnis was praised, a worthy son to Lamon and Myrtale.
All this was pleasing. But then they asked him would he stay the night
Since at first light they planned a sacrifice to Dionysus –
  Dionysus! Every god now Daphnis praised.
  Chloe with Nape, Daphnis with Dryas was to sleep!

61

    They woke next morning to a cold North wind,
But not before, dreaming of Chloe, Daphnis had embraced
And woken Dryas from his sleep. They sacrificed a ram
And Nape kneaded bread as Dryas stoked and blew the fire

    To boil the meat. This was the opportunity
    For Daphnis, taking Chloe by the hand, to lead
        Her out of doors to see the ivy snares.

    Although they caught more birds they still contrived
Alternately to kiss and speak. Thus breathlessly:
'It was because of you I came through all this snow.'

'I know.' 'It's just to see you that I've caught these poor ringdoves.'
'What would you have me do?' 'Remember me.' 'I swore to that
Already in the cave. And when this snow melts I'll return.'
    'The fire in my heart should melt it soon.'

62

    Chloe, like Echo, echoed Daphnis' vows
Until they heard their names called from the house. Reluctantly
They came in from the cold, bringing more birds for Nape's stock.
They offered drops of wine to Dionysus from the bowl;
They put on woven crowns of ivy and began to eat
    And called out loudly Dionysus' name.

    But when the feast was over it was time
For Daphnis to return. They made him take the doves with him
For Lamon and Myrtale's table, since if winter held
And still the ivy bore its generous fruit, they could catch more.
He kissed them all, deftly ensuring Chloe was the last,
So that her kiss would linger on his lips all through the snow.
  And yet he found with Eros' help a dozen ways
  To visit her again before harsh winter's end.

63

    One morning when they woke, it seemed that spring
Already was in progress in the fields, almost as if,
Despite the melting snows, harsh winter had not ever been.
The shepherds brought their flocks again to pasture. Leading them

    Were Daphnis and Chloe, perhaps because they were employed
    By Eros, shepherd of all the world. And soon they ran
        To the Nymphs who stirred now in their melting cave,

    And then to Pan in the shadow of his pine,
    Before they sat beneath their oak tree with their flocks,
    And kissed again at last in spring's pale flowering sun.

Then, wishing to give garlands to the gods, they looked for flowers
And gathered early violets and primrose and daffodils
Which startled the frozen fields. This done, they challenged the nightingales
    Who after winter's silence reviewed their songs.

64

  Sheep were bleating, lambs were skipping, butting,
Suckling at the ewes. Those ewes which had not lambed, the rams
Were chasing heatedly in circles, leaping, trapping them,
While equally the goats were making ardent leaps, the males
In scrimmages and fending off attacks by rival males.
  An old man might be fired to see such sights;

  Then how must Daphnis in his spring and Chloe
Who were filled with love be made more feverish by their flocks?
And as they kissed, he urged that they should try more patiently
That remedy of Philetas requiring them to lie
Together naked. 'But,' cried Chloe, 'What do we actually do?'
'What rams and ewes do. Afterwards how peacefully they graze.'
  But Chloe still had doubts. 'There's something wrong. The sheep
  Don't shed their coats, nor lie down. They're all standing up.'

65

    But Daphnis was convinced. He found a hill
From which the western breeze and sun had melted all its snow,
And brought young grass and flowers. Here they kissed and embraced,
Then cast aside their clothes as if they were beside the spring,

    About to bathe. Yet, filled with great uncertainty,
    Beauty shone unmistakeably but it supplied
        No knowledge or instruction. So they lay

        And lay for many minutes in that bliss
    Of thinking, waiting something more to follow this
    But what they could not tell, who found impediment

At every turn. At last they stood and tried to imitate
The leaping goats but found again the same perplexity.
Daphnis felt shame. He wept aloud that he knew less of love
    Than sheep or goats disporting in the fields.

66

    But, in a neighbouring field, a farmer lived.
His name was Chromis. Somewhat old, he had a younger wife,
Lycanion, who was warm and generous, and elegant,
Since until recently she lived in town. One morning she,
Alert beside her window had observed the goatherd pass,
    Then every evening watched for his return.

    Her heart was set on him. And so, as if
By chance they met. She gave him gifts, some honey in the comb,
A pan flute and a deer-skin purse. They talked but this was all;
She dared not speak of love because she knew that Daphnis loved
The girl he met each morning in the fields. And this she knew
Because she followed him and hid in bushes near the hill
    And, seeing all they did and tried to do in tears,
    Felt sorrow mingle with desire at their distress.

67

    Here was a double opportunity
To kill two willing birds with one delightful stone. And so,
Informing Chromis that she had to see a friend in town,
She openly approached the oak tree where the lovers sat.

    'Oh Daphnis, help me, please. I don't know what to do,'
She cried aloud with tears and wringing of her hands.
    'An eagle carried off my finest goose

    And dropped it in the forest on its way.
I beg you, in the name of Pan and all the Nymphs,
To come with me into the woods.' So Daphnis rose

Immediately and with his shepherd's staff went off with her.
She led him far from Chloe, deep into the darkest glade
And there they sat beside a fountain. Then she said, 'Daphnis!
    Daphnis, the Nymphs have told me everything.'

68

    'They told me how unhappy you have been
And in a dream instructed me to teach you all I can
Of love. They told me of a fire you cannot quench, of tears,
And how you've lain with Chloe on the ground but have not learnt
The calm delights that even sheep and goats can never know.
    I'll teach you. Put yourself into my hands.'

    Daphnis was beside himself with joy;
He promised for her kindness cheeses made from goats' first milk…
She told him to begin with kisses as he had with Chloe,
Then while kissing her to throw his arms strongly about her,
(So far Philetas was right) and lie across her breasts.
Daphnis applied himself and learnt with earnest happiness.
   She taught him until Nature needed no more Art,
   And then her body seemed about him everywhere.

69

    This lesson at an end, Daphnis leapt up
Intent to run with all his new-found knowledge to the field
Where Chloe waited. But Lycanion took his arm. She smiled.
'You've been an excellent pupil, apt and capable. I'm pleased

    To have played a part in guiding you. But there is more
    You still must learn. Your Chloe is an innocent.
    The man who taught me all that I've taught you

    Caused me much pain before he gave me joy,
    And Chloe too, were you to use your strength as you
    Delightfully did with me, would cry with frightened tears.'

Lycanion tenderly embraced him. 'Oh sweet lustrous youth,
Bring Chloe here to this secluded glade and when at first
She cries in pain you'll comfort her and help her bathe her wounds.
    Then Daphnis, in your joys, remember me.'

70

    These warnings weighed on him as he returned,
And strangely coloured his delight at all he'd learned. He paused.
He feared to hurt her. There she sat, with violets in her hair.
He kissed her and embraced her as he had Lycanion.
    She put the crown of violets round his head

    And kissed his hair and called it beautiful,
More beautiful than they. Perhaps it would be wise, despite
His knowledge and his prowess gained today, just for a time,
To be content with all their usual pleasures. So it was
That he invented something about the goose snatched from the claws
Of the eagle in the forest. Chloe then took from her bag
    A piece of fig cake and some bread, and held it out,
    And laughingly fed him like a young bird in a nest.

71

    Nearby, a fishing-boat approached the land.
The wind had dropped. The sailors had to row and as they rowed
They sang in unison to one who led their choruses.
When still in the open sea this pleasant noise could not be heard,

  But as they drew below a cape and in a bay
  Surrounded by a crescent wall of hills, these sounds
    Redoubled, echoing against the shore.

    So Daphnis listened in that windless calm
  To voices and the knock and swathe of oars, heard twice,
  Once from their source, then overlapping these again,

Those land-locked echoes following always in parallel.
But Chloe looked to sea and then beyond the woods, seeking
Some second boat with singing mariners. And Daphnis smiled,
    Returned the crown of violets and explained:

72

'The sound of oars and voices which you hear
A second time within the woods is Echo singing there,
Whose tale I'll tell you now, the fee this kiss returned tenfold.'
Chloe agreed to pay. Daphnis began. 'To one of the Nymphs
A daughter, Echo came. She soon could play the flute and lyre,
    And when she reached your age and beauty, sang

    And danced with the Nymphs. But she avoided males,
Divine or human. Pan, for this and envy of her music,
And wanting that from her she would not give, became enraged,
Inciting shepherds who like dogs and wolves tore her apart.
Each fragment of her body went on singing, and the Nymphs
Hid these in many places in the earth where still they sing.
  And now they imitate whatever sound they hear;
    When Pan himself plays, they prolong his final notes.'

73

    Chloe repaid her debt a hundredfold
When murmuring echoes of his voice confirmed all that he said.
Such kisses crowned in wreaths their summer games. Each day the sun
Embraced the fields more warmly. Daphnis swam each day in streams,

    Chloe found cooling springs. While Daphnis pitched his pipe
    Against the winds that whistled through the pines, she sang
        In playful contest with the nightingales.

    They chased the locusts in their web of noise;
    Grasshoppers with their sound of scything grass they caught.
    In pulsing glades they shook the trees and ate the fruit.

Sometimes again they lay together naked in the field
And slept like this beneath a single goatskin. Yet he feared
To wound her, and held back. But sometimes in his pain he gazed
    Then puzzled her by begging her to dress.

74

    That summer many suitors flocked with gifts
For Dryas, seeking Chloe as a wife. He studied each;
But noble birth deserved a better match. More practical,
His Nape urged him to consent to one or other soon
Before the prize were lost for roses or a gift of fruit
In summer heat. But Dryas still delayed.

    When Daphnis heard of this he wept aloud
And through his tears said he must die, as would his sheep, to lose
A shepherdess like her. He vowed to speak to Dryas too
And Chloe made him confident. But Lamon was not rich
And this made him despair. Myrtale spoke on his behalf
But Lamon thought a shepherdess unsuited for his son.
  Then Daphnis wept again. If only he were rich;
    And in this state he turned once more to the Nymphs for help.

75

Again they came before him in a dream
And, still as beautiful, stood fanned by some hidden breeze.
'The marriage of Chloe is another god's concern, but we
Can help you to win Dryas. You'll remember how the yacht,

Whose mooring rope your goats devoured, was blown away
Far from the land. But what you did not know is that
During the night it foundered on some rocks.

Its cargo all was lost except a purse.
Three thousand drachmas in that purse now lie beneath
The body of a dolphin on your beach. Go there.'

The Nymphs and darkness faded. Daphnis hastened with his flocks,
And after kissing Chloe walked down to the sea. The beach
Was empty, but the smell of dolphin flesh announced the cove;
He found the purse and thanked the Nymphs aloud.

76

    Daphnis now loved the sea as much as land
Because it was his ally and would help to bring him Chloe.
Armed with the purse he ran to Dryas. 'Dryas, give me Chloe
For my wife! I play the pan flute well. I plough and prune
And winnow grain with equal skill. I'm good at planting trees.
    Chloe can tell how well I herd my flocks.

    From fifty goats I now have double that.
I'm young. I live nearby. And just as Chloe had a ewe
To suckle her, my wet-nurse was a goat. So there you see
We are well matched and my accomplishments exceed all those
Who bring you trifling gifts. But Dryas, look! Not only that!
I'm able now to make this handsome gift. Three thousand drachmas –
    All this is yours for Chloe's hand and happiness!
    (But don't say anything of this to Lamon yet.)'

77

    Dryas agreed at once as Nape smiled,
And Daphnis stayed with her and drove the oxen threshing wheat,
While Dryas hastened to his neighbour Lamon in the strange
And curious role of asking for his son in marriage. There

    He found them quite depressed. Their crops seemed scarcely more
    Than all the seed they'd sown. He sympathised at length,
        Then hurried on to offer Chloe's hand.

    Many fine suitors he'd refused. But then,
    (By Pan!) so sure was he that this was meant to be
    That he himself would pay a dowry. Daphnis he admired,

The two were fond companions, the gods had smiled…et cetera.
So Lamon could not plead his poverty but still believed
Daphnis was worthy of a better prize. 'Dryas,' he said,
    'We are agreed. But let us wait till autumn.'

78

    Dryas walked thoughtfully along those paths,
Which snowbound Daphnis had for love traversed, towards his house.
Lamon had said, 'Remember Daphnis is above us all.'
And Dryas now began to wonder who this boy might be.
Protected by a she-goat, smiled upon by Providence!
    And, unlike Lamon, handsome as a tree.

    And those three thousand drachmas, what of them?
A goatherd would be fortunate to have three thousand pears!
But if he were abandoned and protected by the Nymphs,
If Lamon found him, were there tokens lying at his side
Like those that lay by Chloe? If this were so, what could it mean?
These pleasant thoughts and dreams contented Dryas on his way.
    Once home, and pleased at Daphnis making flour, he said,
    To Daphnis' joy, 'An autumn wedding, son-in-law.'

79

  Elated by these words, Daphnis leapt up
And ran, swifter than thought to Chloe who was making cheese.
He told her everything. Gladly they kissed amongst the pails,
Openly like man and wife. Then Daphnis shared the work.

  He milked, he filled the cheese press, then he held the lambs
  And kids beneath their mothers. At last, happy and tired,
    They washed and ate and went in search of fruit.

  One apple tree was bare. On the highest branch
  A single apple shone like gold, fragrant as wine
  And out of reach. Daphnis was fired by pride and love

And clambered for the swaying fruit. He ran with it to Chloe.
'This is the prize which Aphrodite won for beauty. Now
It's yours.' Gently he placed this golden sphere between her breasts;
  Then tenderly she took him in her arms.

Book Four

80

Now, ever since the Methymnean siege of coastal lands,
    Rumours had spread that Lamon's city lord,
    The master of all these orchards, flocks and fields
Would soon arrive to see if his estates in these attacks

Had suffered damage. Lamon swept the yards and dredged the spring,
And then surveyed the garden which of all near Mytilene
    Was thought most beautiful: a wealth of trees,
Apple and pear and myrtle, pomegranate, fig, with vines

    Enclustered through the leaves with darkening grapes;
Beyond these, cypresses and laurels, pines and plane trees grew
And over them a wreath of ivy trailed its glistening berries.

    A dry-stone hedge surrounding these gave calm
    And order to the place. Although these trunks were spaced
At equal intervals, their leaves formed one great mass.

81

    As well as ordered groves and tangling vines,
Flowers in plots and borders – some, like rose and hyacinth,
Requiring human hand, and some which earth herself brought forth,
    Dark violets, pale narcissus – multiplied.

    Lamon looked proudly there: in summer, shade;
In spring, abundance; fruit in autumn, everywhere delight.
From where he stood, the meadows could be seen with grazing flocks
And to the south, the sea, where ships were sailing tranquilly.
Then at the measured centre of the grove in dappled shade
    A temple and an altar stood, a maze

    Of paintings praising Dionysus: Semele
Is giving birth; pale Ariadne sleeps. And Pentheus
Is torn apart, Lycurgus chained, amazed Tyrrhenians
    Are pictured being changed to dolphins in the foam.

82

And on all sides there ran a frieze of satyrs treading grapes
    And Bacchantes dancing. Seated on the rock,
    His hooves above the spray, his curving horns
Amongst the dancers, Pan played music honouring Dionysus.

Such was the garden, Lamon's pride, which now he trimmed and trained
And watered every morning from a spring called Daphnis' Spring
    (Its first discoverer). He placed a wreath
On Dionysus and the pantheon attending him.

    Lamon was also anxious that the goats
Should, under Daphnis' care, look fat and fleet. Daphnis
Was confident. The fifty goats with which he had begun

    Were more than doubled. Not a single one
    Had been surrendered to the wolves. And they were plump;
Because of Daphnis' care they looked like fleecy sheep.

83

    Yet Daphnis wanted everything to be
Perfect, immaculate, so that his master would approve
His marriage soon to Chloe, she who was immaculate
        And perfect in his eyes. And so he took

        His goats at dawn to a particular field
Where sun and shade and air and grass best suited them. As well,
He brought new pails and bowls and fresh large baskets for the cheese,
And even in his zeal groomed all the goats. He oiled their horns
And polished them and washed and combed their coats until they looked
        Like goats fit to attend great Pan himself.

    Chloe neglected her own sheep to work with him
To preen and polish every goat. And so assiduously
They laboured at their tasks together, they allowed themselves
        Only a modicum of kisses as they toiled.

84

But now a messenger named Eudromos arrived from town:
> The grapes must now be harvested, the wine
> Drawn from the press. And then, to celebrate

Those vintage rites their master would with ceremony attend.

The vines were stripped, the grapes brought to the press, the sweet new wine
Poured into jars. Some clustered grapes, their frosted bloom intact
> Were carefully set aside with vines and leaves
> To show the cloistered city something of the country's joys.

> The jars were filled and Eudromos could leave.

And Daphnis gave him gifts – firm cheeses and a late-born kid,
A fleece which he as emissary should wear in winter's cold;

> All were reminders of the goatherd's skill.
> The two embraced and Eudromos vowed that he would
> Speak well of Daphnis with their master in the town.

85

    Clear days brought Daphnis to the fields with Chloe,
Yet a shadow seemed to fall across them, one which neither tree
Nor cloud explained. For Daphnis feared and Chloe with him feared
    The master whom they had not ever seen.

    Perhaps when he arrived they would be told
Their dreams of marriage were just dreams. And they embraced
So closely that it seemed they were one undividing branch.
But when they stepped apart, that shadow fell across their lives;
Again they embraced to escape unknown fears as if they could
    Hide in each other's arms from all the world.

    But something else now happened which would bring them pain.
A jealous suitor, Lampis, wanting Chloe still, enraged,
And thinking how to damage Daphnis in his master's eyes,
    At night despoiled the garden, tearing and trampling flowers.

86

He tore and trampled with those borders Daphnis' hopes, then left
    Unseen. When Lamon came and saw next day
    This devastated grove he tore his clothes
And cried aloud to all the gods. Myrtale ran and Daphnis

Left his goats. While many flowers lay tousled on the ground,
The bees still came upon them; here and there some calyx still
    Held pollen and their buzzing drone was like
A dirge in Lamon's ears. He cried out pitifully, 'Alas!

    For all the roses broken in their beds,
The violets pressed into clay, the hyacinths, their stems
Tattered and torn. This autumn there will be no garlands. Spring

    Will come and still will be as barren here.
    Oh Dionysus, could you not pity these flowers?
    And when our master comes what will he say of this?'

87

    When Night at last came, covering these sad sights,
And still those mourners were lamenting, Eudromos returned.
To Daphnis now his message was a knell. In three days time
    Their master would be walking in this grove,

    Would see the abundant signs of their neglect,
Of Daphnis' goats let wander recklessly; Daphnis reproached
Is banished, never more to see his Chloe's weeping face,
Or worse, with Lamon, hanged. But Eudromos had more to say.
Their master's son, named Astylus, would soon arrive. 'Perhaps,'
    Said Eudromos, 'If I can talk to him –

For we are foster-brothers – then his father may
Be influenced by him in what he sees. At least I'll try.'
Next day young Astylus arrived on horseback. With him came
    An older man, Gnathon, who greeted Daphnis warmly.

88

Then everyone began to speak to Astylus at once.
      Lamon knelt down and with Myrtale begged
        That he might keep them from his father's rage;
And Daphnis told him everything, suggesting that he come

With them to see the trampled beds with his own eyes. He went,
And walked along the rows and listened sympathetically,
      Then raised their trampled hopes by promising
To intercede. He would explain that his own horses were,

      While tethered there, alarmed and suddenly
Impelled by fear to break their reins and gallop wild-eyed, leap
And tangle ordered trellises beneath their hooves. This would,

      He said, remove all thought of their neglect.
Then grateful Daphnis ran with gifts of kids and cheeses, hens
With all their broods, grapes on the vine, fruits with their boughs.

89

    In praise of Astylus these shepherds brought
A jar of that most precious wine on earth, the wine of Lesbos,
Fragrant as the air on sloping fields which smell of thyme.
    Then Astylus replied to praise with praise

    And well pleased with events went hunting hares.
But brooding Gnathon stayed behind and poured himself more wine
And looked at Daphnis as he drank. He overfilled his cup.
The more he drank the more he gazed at Daphnis openly,
Finding this rustic so enticing that he planned to make
    A union of the country with the town.

He followed Daphnis to the field pretending there
An interest in the goats when all the time his one desire
Was Daphnis. Honeyed words about the pastoral flute ensued
    And his fervent wish that Daphnis play that instrument.

90

But soon the drunken Gnathon cast aside all subtlety
    And pointing to a pair of rutting goats
   Proposed that he and Daphnis play the goat
Like them, and clumsily embraced him. Daphnis was surprised

And puzzled. When at last he thought he understood and said
He'd never seen two bucks or rams or roosters doing that,
    The boor tried bribes. His influence
    With Astylus could win for Daphnis freedom from this life

   Of drudgery with goats and pails and fields.
And when this failed he tried to have his way with clumsy force;
They struggled until Daphnis threw him down amongst the goats,

   And ran away, still startled, from his flocks.
   Unchastened, Gnathon followed him in time to see
   Dionysophanes and all his entourage.

91

    The bustle and confusion – servants, maids,
Supplies, the baggage animals, and all those ceremonies
Which must attend renown – frustrated Gnathon for a time.
    Instead he learnt by heart a rambling speech

    In which he would depict his desperate love
For Daphnis and through Astylus and his father have his way.
Dionysophanes was tall, grey-haired and handsome, and
Despite his wealth both generous and fair. The following day,
When the countryside was revelling in the sun and fragrant airs,
    He sacrificed to all the country gods,

  Then, with his wife Cleariste, saw the estates. The fields
Were newly ploughed, the vines after the vintage trimmed and trained.
All this was warmly praised. Even the grove seemed beautiful,
  And Astylus explained the lack of trailing flowers.

92

Adjourning next to the field to see the goatherd and his goats,
>   They did not notice Chloe run in fright
>   Into the copse until the crowds were gone.
But Daphnis was superb, a goatskin tied around his waist,

And statuesque, with unweaned kids held in his arms. Like this
Apollo must have looked as herdsman to Laomedon.
>   Proud Lamon praised his diligence and skill
And stressed the power of Daphnis' music over all his herds.

>   Cleariste, intrigued, asked Daphnis now to play.
He sat them on a gentle slope as in a theatre. Then
Beneath the oak he played a low note. All the goats stood still.

>   He played a grazing tune and so they grazed.
>   A gentle tune and down they lay. A strident note
>   And to the woods they ran to hide, fearing a wolf.

93

    And finally he played an anaclete,
Recalling them. Out from the woods they leaped and ran as one,
And gathered round his feet. Like all her company, Cleariste
    Was so amazed she promised him rich gifts,

    And praised his music and his pristine goats.
At lunch, Daphnis and Chloe shared confections from the town
And Daphnis felt fresh hope that he and Chloe now might wed.
But Gnathon, even more inflamed by Daphnis with his goats,
Drew Astylus aside: 'Alas! You see before you now
    A broken man. I once loved nothing more

    Than eating at your table, drinking fine old wine
I thought your cooks finer than all the boys of Mytilene.
Yet now I'm dazzled by the sun that shines in Daphnis' eyes.
    I swear to you, by Dionysus, I am lost!'

94

When Gnathon through his tears proclaimed the ennobling change
        That love for Daphnis brought, and cried his name,
        And darkly dwelt on his own suicide,
Should this great love be unrequited, Astylus was swayed,

And said he'd intercede. His father might perhaps agree
To make Daphnis their servant in the town. 'But why,' he laughed,
        Voicing some doubt, 'a rustic goatherd boy?
And aren't goats rather aromatic?' Gnathon now resumed

        His practised rhetoric in praise of love.
'Love does not choose its object. Men have loved a tree or river
Or devouring beast. But Daphnis is beautiful – that hair

        Like hyacinths, those colouring cheeks. Besides,
    When Zeus took Ganymede he was amongst his herds,
    As was Anchises when he lay with Aphrodite.'

95

    'What sophistry!' laughed Astylus, yet promised
Still to ask his father. By good fortune, Eudromos
Had overheard all this, and fearing lest a drunkard prey
        On beauty, ran to Lamon with the tale.

    While Daphnis vowed to trust the gods and flee
Or die with Chloe, Lamon called Myrtale from the house
And begged them all to listen: 'I am old. The time has come
For secrets to be shared. Whatever consequences follow,
I'll tell them how our Daphnis was exposed then found by us,
        Suckled by goats, protected by the gods,

    And with what tokens of his noble birth. And then
That parasite will know what kind he has presumed to love.'
But, meanwhile, Astylus had found his father generous,
        Believing city life a just reward for Daphnis.

96

These two contending forces met at Dionysus' shrine.
    Lamon was summoned to be told the news
    That Daphnis had been raised to high estate
To serve the house of Astylus instead of goats

(And two goatherds appointed in his place). But Lamon spoke
And on his words hung Daphnis' fate: 'My Master, hear the truth.
    I am the father of no man. Daphnis
I found as a baby in a cave, suckled by goats, protected

    By the gods, and with him in that bed there were
Such tokens of a noble birth as made us always praise
The goat that nurtured him. In fact, when recently she died,

    I buried her beside this shrine. In short
    By virtue of his birth Daphnis deserves a fate
    More fitting than as Gnathon's woman in the town.'

97

He paused. Gnathon who swore and threatened him,
Dionysophanes rebuked severely with a glance.
He questioned Lamon who told all his tale again. At this
    A hush of expectation seized the crowd.

    Myrtale ran into the house to find
Those tokens which had waited every day of Daphnis' life
So that he now could choose to live. Dionysophanes
Received the parcel, opened it and gasped as it divulged
The cloak of Tyrian purple, the knife, the brooch of beaten gold;
    And Cleariste too cried out, 'Oh, Fates! Great Zeus!

The very articles we sent out with our son!'
'And was it not towards these fields we sent Sophrone then
That dark and humid afternoon?' 'The child is our own son!
    This Daphnis is the goatherd of his father's goats!'

98

Through all these tears of joy, their subject, Daphnis, stood apart,
    Afraid of being taken to the town,
    And did not understand when Astylus
With echoing cries and calling of his name ran towards him.

Daphnis turned and ran, believing still he was condemned
To leave his fields and flocks and Chloe. Nor did he yet know
    That Astylus pursuing was his brother,
So that he ran towards a cliff meaning to hurl himself

    Into the sea, lost to that very world
Which had just found him. Astylus saw this and stopped. He saw
Daphnis uncertain at the brink. He called, 'Daphnis! You are

    My brother and my father's son. We've seen the tokens.
    Turn and look and see these faces as they come
Laughing with joy towards you. By the Nymphs, it's true.'

99

    So on those cliffs where calmly, far below,
The changing shallows moved, they gathered round him. Joyfully
Each one embraced him – Astylus, the servants, all amazed
        To find the gods had plaited such a braid.

    But in his parents' arms he lingered long
Already knowing in his heart whatever might be new,
And for a moment which spread outward like a field, forgot
All he had been and even Chloe. But soon they left the cliff
And in the cottage, dressed in strange and sumptuous clothes, he heard
        His father's tale of what seemed like a dream.

    'My sons, I married young and fortune soon had brought
A son and then a daughter and then Astylus. Our cup
Seemed filled. So when another child arrived, we sent him out,
        As was the custom, for the gods there to dispose.'

100

'Sophrone was directed to these fields. This now we know.
    And even as the gods preserved you here
    They took from us our eldest son and daughter,
Both on a single day. But as so often is the case,

The gods resolve a synthesis made out of men's mistakes
More happily than ever they could otherwise achieve;
    And Providence unites my sons at last.
Daphnis, lose your reproaches in our love. And Astylus,

    A brother's love is more than rich reward
For sharing your inheritance. Now from those vast reserves,
This manor and its well-trained herd of goats we freely give

    To Lamon and Myrtale.' At these words,
Daphnis leapt up exclaiming, 'Oh! The goats! The goats!
It's noon and I'm neglecting them. They need their drink.'

101

    That Daphnis now the owner of these fields
Should hurry off to move his goats or take them to the spring
Seemed humorous and touching. Everyone cried, 'Daphnis! Stay!
    Let someone else attend to that. You're free.'

    So, anxious still about his goats, he joined
His family in a sacrifice to Zeus the great Preserver,
Then was honoured at the feast which overflowed the house
Into the fields. But wretched Gnathon was not there. Alone,
Reviled, he trembled in the shades of Dionysus' shrine,
    While wine and waterfowl and honey cakes

    Made festive every visitor. Amongst them came
Dryas who warmly sought out Daphnis in the joyful crowd,
But found him with a puzzled air of loss instead of gain
    As all his pastoral possessions he farewelled.

102

To all the gods these dearly loved and ancient articles
        He sadly offered: first, to the Nymphs his pails
        Made from a cypress fallen near their cave;
To Dionysus in his grove a goatskin coat; to Pan

A shepherd's staff on which he leaned for many summer days.
And yet such things bearing the marks of long familiar use
        May often seem more valuable than new
And glittering gifts.And so in tears he filled the pails with milk,

        One last sad time, and held the polished staff
And wore the coat and played the flute again, and called each goat
By name and talked to it. And then he drank from the cool spring

        In which so often he had drunk before.
He lingered still where once with Chloe he had played
        And bathed and held her long; and now he longed for her.

103

    Meanwhile, alone, neglected Chloe sat
In tears beside her quiet, distant sheep. Beneath their oak
She spoke aloud. 'Alas! For Daphnis has forgotten me.
    Now he has dreams of marrying someone rich.

    If only I had let him swear by the Nymphs
Instead of by these goats, for he's deserting them and will desert
His mournful Chloe who, a life ago, lived in his love.
How cool the spring in which we bathed, which once seemed like a flame.
How pale the sun at noon which once seemed shadowless to us.
    Now Daphnis finds his mother's servant-girls

Are prettier than I and they have captured him.'
Just then as Chloe sat debating with the silent sheep
Lampis, assuming that his rival now would quit the field,
    Seized Chloe and with local help abducted her.

104

The plan had been to win consent from Dryas but the news
        Of Chloe's cries soon reached him. He in turn
        Sought Daphnis who lamented all his loss:
'Oh wretched freedom! What dark gods devised this fruitless change?

When yesterday I was a herdsman, every day I saw
And spoke with Chloe, kissed and held her. Now I'm rich and free
        And hateful Lampis has her in his bed.'
Standing in the shadows, Gnathon overheard all this

        And saw the chance to win back favour. So
He ran to Astylus and taking several more young men
They strode to Lampis' house, arriving just in time to free

        Pale frightened Chloe and to give the thief
    His just reward. Lampis at last escaped their blows
And Gnathon conducted Chloe back to Daphnis' arms.

105

    This Chloe like a flower which blooms again
The rain of Daphnis' gaze refreshed. This Chloe lost but found
Let Gnathon make his peace with Daphnis. Still the task remained
    To tell his father of their plans. They feared

    To risk finality by voicing them.
But Dryas disagreed. The time had come to speak. And when
Dionysophanes and Cleariste sat with Astylus
He said, 'Like Lamon, I confess a secret I've not shared
With anyone. My Chloe here is not my daughter. She
    Like Daphnis lay abandoned in a cave,

    Protected by the Nymphs and suckled by a ewe.
Her beauty must confirm her origins, as these must do –
These tokens richly strange to us, we found with her. Take them.
    Perhaps nobility makes her a match for Daphnis.'

106

Dionysophanes gave due regard to this remark.
    He looked at Daphnis brimming with young tears
    And recognised himself from days long gone.
He saw grave Chloe's gaze, at which, with her, he loved his son.

But now the matter of the tokens. These he held in turn:
The anklets made of gold, the girdle woven in gold thread,
    The gilded shoes. He smiled and said to her,
'Be happy for my sake. You have a husband now. And soon

    By means of these which Dryas has preserved
I'll find a mother and a father who will love you still
As I love both my sons.' Cleariste took Chloe in her arms

    Then took her to another room to dress
In clothes of bridal white (on which point Daphnis made
His father smile: 'A virgin? Yes. I know for sure.')

107

    Her radiance now seemed focused like the sun
Through glass, which makes a dazzling, dancing beam of light and heat.
Dryas and Nape voiced their admiration for this grace:
        'Such beauty clearly was not born of us.'

    And others called her daughter of the Nymphs,
Stepped from their peristyle and cave, her hair like theirs, afloat
And here and there in crossing braids, her face as bright, her eyes
Mysterious even to Daphnis. And to everyone
She seemed the Earth itself, pristine in early spring or snow,
        Familiar yet strangely redolent

Of something we have known but cannot ever find
And know is always close to us. Dionysophanes
Spoke gently. Soon she must prepare to leave for Mytilene
    To find her parents and be married to his son.

108

Chloe, like Daphnis, bade farewell to all the accoutrements
    Of vines and herds which had so sweetly bound
    Her to the fields. Her fleecy cloak, her pipes,
Her pails and buckets – all she consecrated to the gods.

She poured a bowl of wine into the spring beside whose bank
She had been suckled and in which with Daphnis she had bathed.
    She played a pastorale to her sad flock
And garlanded the grave where that propitious ewe now lay.

    But after further gifts and courtesies
They left. They travelled through the woods and over fields, past streams
And villages which marvelled at these splendid carriages,

    Their horses all caparisoned in gilt,
    And equipage exotic and mysterious.
    Night dews were rising when their caravan arrived.

109

    Amongst the crowds who came the following day
Were many ladies who, on seeing Chloe, prayed to the gods
That they be thought the mother of so beautiful a child
    But in this quest again Eros prevailed.

    In sleep Dionysophanes was shown
The Nymphs attending Eros in a trellised garden. Light
Was fringed with silver where he moved. He smiled and joined the hands
Of Daphnis and Chloe, then casting down his quiver and his bow
Proposed a banquet for the citizens of Mytilene:
    The wine is poured; the tokens are displayed,

A father will be seated at this table. So
The finest foods were brought from sea and land and marsh and stream,
Whatever might seem rich, entrancing, as might befit
    The joyful naming of a daughter and a bride.

110

The wine was served and then a silver tray which held those treasures
        Passed before each guest. These shreds of gold,
        Like candles in a window waiting still,
Brought no response until at last a merchant, Megacles

Cried out in wonderment, 'Oh let the gods be merciful.
Were these, the tokens of my daughter, scattered to the winds
        Or did the gods preserve her with them? Who
Amongst this company can tell me of my daughter's fate?'

        Dionysophanes cried, 'First, tell us
When last you held these tokens and the child.' And Megacles
Replied: 'I could not run the risk of poverty for her.

        I gave her to the Nymphs. But when, too late,
        I was both rich and childless, then the gods mocked me
        In dreams, making a ewe the mother of my child.'

111

  At this Cleariste brought Chloe, radiant, white,
Uncertain, grave, hesitant yet serene. Without a word
She gazed at Megacles and Rhode and then embraced them both.
  Dionysophanes at length declared:

  'As I with Daphnis, on the very day
You find her you must give her up again to Eros who
Protected them.' And Megacles observing now their grace,
And seeing something of the beauty of the gods in them
Agreed most willingly. Then Daphnis spoke: 'Chloe and I
  Are yearning to return to Lamon's grove

  To celebrate with you, our new-found families,
Our marriage feast there in the presence of the Nymphs. We miss
Our sheep and goats here in the town. We long to hear
  The breeze in Pan's tree tell us we are man and wife.'

112

And thus the town moved to the countryside a second time,
> Delighting in the weather and the air
> Which seemed itself to carry from the Past
Its fleeting tokens on the breeze which all might recognise.

They sat on banks of leaves outside the cave. They ate and sang.
They danced. And everyone was there: Nape and Dryas, Lamon
> And Myrtale, Philetas and his sons,
Some relatives of Dorcon, Chromis and Lycanion,

> And even Lampis, now forgiven. The goats
Browsed too, disquieting some city guests. Tall tales were told
Of harvest times; and reapers sang some questionable songs,

> While Philetas played dancing melodies.
> Chloe and Daphnis kissed. Then Daphnis called the goats
> And fed them succulent leaves and grasped them by the horns.

113

    For many years Daphnis and Chloe would,
From love and not necessity, pursue these pastoral joys,
Serving the Nymphs, great Pan and Eros. Thus, to their baby boy
    They brought a nurturing she-goat. Then a ewe

    In milk they gave to suckle their baby girl.
In time they built a simple shrine to Eros in the cave,
And through the years this rustic way of life grew old with them.
But that was still to come. And on this warm and fragrant night
The guests now led them to the bridal bed, some piping, some
    In raucous song. At last they were alone.

    They lay together naked, and embraced and kissed
And thought no more of sleep than owls do. Daphnis did those things
Lycanion had taught him. And Chloe learned at last that all
    They'd known beneath the trees had been mere children's games.

www.ingramcontent.com/pod-product-compliance
Lightning Source LLC
Chambersburg PA
CBHW070915080526
44589CB00013B/1302